But You said, "Yes!"

DISCOVER THE POWER IN STAYING COMMITTED IN MARRIAGE

Shanise L. Ollie

Shanise L. Ollie

shaniseollie@gmail.com

Flint, MI 48507

www.shaniseolliejourneyto30.com

ISBN-13:
978-1530851171

ISBN-10:
1530851173

Printed in the United States of America
Copyright Information

But You said, "Yes"

Cover Designer: Ollie Design Compay

Photographer: Timothy pAULE ™

Styled by: SV Style

Make-up Artist: Erika Dunn

.

CONTENTS

Acknowledgements

This book is dedicated to women everywhere; may we overcome by the word of our testimonies and being truthfully honest in who God has called us to be. Being a wife may not be easy but where lack abides, grace abides much more. Never give up the pursuit to being the wife God called you to be. To my mother Francine Mitchell, grandmother Priscilla Stokes, Aunt Sheila Vaughn, Aunt Amy Stokes, and best friend Kori Coleman. Thank you ladies for always believing in my dreams, and pushing me into my purpose. Thank you for being Godly examples of a wife and mother. I thank God for your lives. I pray that I continue to make you proud.

I would also like to thank my father Garold A. Mitchell, thank you for showing me what it looks like for a real man to serve his family. Thank you for your endless sacrifices that have stretched far beyond into my adulthood. To my "Cuz" Kevin Brooks thank

you for inspiring, and always speaking into my life. You and your

family have been a blessing to mine, and mean so much to us.

To my husband, Quandrel Ollie thank you for providing me the

space and opportunity to grow as a wife, and giving me the space

to pursue my passion, and live out God's purpose for my life.

You've always pushed me, encouraged me, strengthened me, and

loved me just the way I was. I love you! Thank you

CHAPTER 1

THE BEGINNING OF IT ALL

Everyone is watching. He gets down on one knee, and from his pocket retrieves *the box*. Not just *a* box, but *"the"* box; the one most women everywhere eagerly dream of receiving. All eyes are on the two of you, as everyone in the room -- and he -- awaits your answer. You say it: "Yes! I will marry you!" Now the *real* journey begins.

You see, it all started the day we said yes. It blows my mind now, after years of marriage, when I think of all the crucial misconceptions many of us have about marriage before we enter into the union. I could see it very vividly in my mind what I believed marriage would be. Endless days and endless nights of time spent staring into each other's eyes, or the time we'd spend sitting by candle light on date nights. We would live in our dream home, work in our dream careers and live life happily without a financial care in the world. I can't forget the attributes that I imagined my husband would have. He would understand my needs and wants without me even having to specifically communicate them; basically finishing my sentences. And, of course, there would be endless elements of romantic gestures such as flowers, cards, and gifts. But the truth of the matter is, some of my expectations were unrealistic for the specific encounters I would experience in my own lessons of love and marriage. If you can relate to feeling let down, confused or just plain lied to about married life, this book is for you.

See, I came from a family where I was surrounded by marriages that I thought were successful. But what does a successful marriage really look like? Is it the years spent married? Or is it the perspective one has of his or her own happiness? Honestly, we have no clue what others endure to accomplish the title of happily ever after. I viewed certain elements from marriages around me, like my parents who have been married now

for thirty-two

years, as well as two sets of grandparents who were married for

50+ years, and thought I understood what marriage took. My

parents made it look so easy.

.

I never experienced seeing my parents argue. Both of my

parents worked good jobs to provide for me and my siblings, and

for the most part they always seemed happy and very loving

toward each other. I never remember us not having what we

needed or sometimes wanted. I saw my father work hard to show

my mother she was very valuable to him.   There was one moment

in my life that I now realize was my father's way of teaching me a

valuable lesson about how a man should treat a woman. It was

Mother's Day, and our church was selling flowers. My father not

only purchased some for my mother, but also purchased one for

my sister and me. It is these types of gestures that allow girls from

a tender young age to generate conceptions about how good it feels

to be treated special by someone you love. I truly felt special that day, and that was where it all began.

I believe God puts certain elements in our lives as a foundation. That foundation will serve as a port to draw from in our own circumstances. It will be filled with both the good and the bad of whatever your experiences may include. It's important to know that no one's marriage will mirror another's. But the special factor in all of this is who God is creating through the shadows of particular occurrences you experience within your own marriage. God is always trying to show us something; in most instances it's about who we are at the root, and who He wants us to be in the bloom. So when I thought I was being misled by others' happily ever after, I was just being exposed to elements that would help me build toward the pursuit of a loving marriage.

The media plays devil's advocate to the realities of the challenges marriage brings by its portrayal of "Happily Ever After. Rarely does it focus on the challenges that will, without exception, follow "I do" in every marriage. I'm not saying there aren't glorious days of wonder, sparks, butterflies, and pure bliss, because they surely exist. However, it also comes hand-in-hand with a lot of hard work, and dedication.

So, yes, before marriage, I had a fictional picture of the union firmly planted in my mind, maybe embedded there, by one too many chick flicks; or maybe I just wanted to believe in magical endings. In hindsight, the fact that I was so easily misled would be laughable. In reality I wasn't even close to being alone in my naivety. Making the decision to go from feeling the way that I was, to taking control of whether or not I had a happy marriage started with an epiphany.

It was one day during my first year of marriage when reality set in. I realized that our lives had gotten busy. We both worked, and as our responsibilities began to flourish, the time we had to spend with each other began to diminish. We began to build our family and the pressures of our financial security increasingly weighed on our relationship. These were storms that I had never weathered, and quite frankly prayed would never be my story. But let me tell you, real life happens, and when it does, you can either learn and grow, or get in the fast lane toward being unhappy.

I heard a very profound notion by Bishop McClendon of Oxygen's television show, "Preacher's of L.A." He explained that it is increasingly harder for people to get married before the age of thirty, because most men aren't cemented in their career or accomplishments. And right around that thirty-year mark, when men start to make that shift, most women get lost in that same shift. They don't take the time to realize the change and how to make the transition with him. This was a redefining moment for me. It really caused me to look at the type of wife I really was.

What type of wife was I really? What part of myself was I

willing to sacrifice or compromise in order to be an intricate, cohesive part of my marriage? If we actually took the time to scale back and do a self-check, and really evaluate what type of partner we truly are, how much stronger and more spiritually sound would our marriages be? Up until that TV moment I had thought about all the things I needed from my husband, and that led to me slowly abandon my willingness to serve him through life's transitions. This realization immediately made me picture my savior's sacrifice, dying a brutal death to serve me. Even when I turned away; even when I lied, cheated or disobeyed, He still pursued me. What a great depiction of love. What greater love is there than a man who would lay down his life? I asked myself if I had followed Christ's example of sacrifice. Unfortunately I had to be honest with myself in answering no .In fact, I hadn't even come close.

This is where my journey to confront my selfishness began; it put me in a mental space that forced me to examine what I had said "yes" to. If we took the time to scale back and do a self-check, and evaluate what type of partner we are, how much stronger would our marriages be? I have come to the conclusion that all of us can and should look inside of ourselves and brutally evaluate the type of partner we are. By making changes, we can all enjoy the strength of a marriage that comes from laying aside our own will and serving our partner as we would God.

I have found that this strategy allows me to serve my husband more graciously, and love him a little more unconditionally and unselfishly each day.

I began an intimate pursuit to become a more understanding wife. Let me explain what I mean by this. There are so many mechanics that go into learning the nuances of someone else's personality, quirks and ways. I'm not sure if most of us -- unprovoked -- take the time to consider all of these details about ourselves, making it that much harder to teach others why we are the way that we are. And that's crucial because our upbringing, our preferences and all of the other little details that make us, *"us"* determine how we relate to others; especially our spouses.

This is why I suggest that the first place to start, before you try to figure out what makes your spouse tick, is to go on a journey of self-discovery, exploring even (and maybe especially) the dark places we've been in our lives and the dark thoughts that have crept through our minds and into our marriages. When I began to analyze myself, I realized that those dark thoughts are kind of like pesky bed bugs that find their way into our suitcases while we're on vacation. While you sleep peacefully at night, those little boogers? are feasting away on your flesh. Next thing you know you're back at home, dumping the mattress you bought years ago with the intention of keeping it for the long haul, right into the dumpster. I've seen this slow, insidious process take place in the marriages of many well-meaning people.

Personal issues and struggles slowly and silently tear away

at our "inner flesh" from the time we meet our spouses. Just as we get comfortable at home, our inner pests rear their ugly little heads and turn our marital plans upside down. One day you're contemplating your golden anniversary, and the next, you're worried your marriage is about to be thrown into the dumpster! How did this happen right underneath our noses? You thought you'd be together forever, but now it looks like the path you're on is headed in only one direction: divorce court.

Before it was too late for us, I decided to do whatever I could to clear the pests out of my marriage. I knew I did not want our story to end with divorce; and I don't want yours to either so, my suggestion to you is to dig deep into the inner workings of yourself and your spouse to see how those details affect your marriage. We will discuss that in the chapter called "Bag Lady." As you dig deep, don't forget to open up space to allow God to do his work. Sometimes it's easy to forget that we can rely on God to prune us, and accompany us through our journey of healing.

What a scary moment for me! The errors of my ways became frighteningly apparent to me. My heart broke with the realization that although I depended on grace for myself, I hadn't been generous enough to give it in return. As I sat back and examined my actions I saw three major issues.

#1. Not handling his heart with care. Most women will skip right over this one, and say, "I got this one nailed." But again -- in many instances -- we don't. When a man gives his heart to a woman, it's serious business that should not be taken lightly. A lot of men struggle to let down their guard enough to be fully vulnerable to a woman and, in many cases; you'd never know it.

A man can get married and stay married for years, but -- often unconsciously or unintentionally -- never give you his heart completely. Past rejections and trust issues are often to blame when men keep their hearts under lock and key. Past relationships with all women -- including mothers, sisters, and especially, exes, -

- greatly influence whether they're eager or reluctant about love. Their past relationships usually offer clear insight into how they navigate around their emotional needs in the present.

While it's extremely helpful to understand your man, I'll offer a cautionary word of advice; before you go digging around in his past, trying to spot his defenses and break them down, I encourage you to ask yourself an important question first; "are you deserving of his full and complete trust?"

We are all fragile and should be handled with care. When it comes to your marriage, are you viewing him in a loving way? As a treasured gift, God gave up his only son in order to save us from sin. He sacrificed his own flesh and blood to prove His love for us. God is God, and God alone doesn't have to prove anything to us. But even God pursued our love by proving His own devotion through Jesus' sacrifice.

What makes you think that your pursuit of your husband's affections should be any different? Sometimes, we are dealing with men who have never experienced the opportunity to know or come in contact with a successful marriage. So how can someone offer that, if they never saw a clear example of what a biblical exchange of love looks like? My marriage is an opportunity for me to show that I feel honored to have my husband's heart so completely, more fully than any other woman had. It was an opportunity to demonstrate and experience what I view as the greatest of all pursuits: love.

#2. The way I listened. Let me just say this right up front, loud and clear -- in most instances, women love to talk. Yes you! I know I do. With that said, many of us *DO NOT* listen as much as we should. And even if you're not a talker, it still takes practice to make your partner feel heard, which is essential if you don't want him to completely tune you out when you're talking.

A big part of helping someone feel that you're really listening is to first identify what goals they have in the conversation. Unlike many women, who may just need to talk and be heard, men are usually looking to boil down the conversation to its essence. In other words, they want you to get to the point.

There's always more to most interactions then the obvious. When you look at him, try to see the man you know he is called to be, and not simply the man he is in the present moment. It's a hard thing to do; believe me, I know. However, this is where I remind you of the reasons you married this man; which hopefully goes beyond him being "fine," or having that good job and that sexy physique. If you need motivation to go deeper than those reasons, refer to the Bible; specifically 1 Samuel 16:7, which says, *"Truly, God does not see what man sees, for man looks at the outward appearance, but the LORD sees the heart."*

If you want to love the man God gave you as God intended,

then start by using your words (or, in some cases -- sparing your words) in a way that enhances his innermost being. What works for me when I'm tempted to deal harshly with my husband is to say to myself "Now you can either speak to the failure of this man, or you can speak life to his future." This is easier said than done, but most rewarding when put into action because we know that actions speak louder than words. So listen intently, and with the mind of Christ.

#3. The way I dealt with his mind. Do you really know your role as the woman in your man's life? I once heard a great speaker, (my pastor, Timothy R. Stokes), say: "You're the influencer." God keeps showing me what an amazing job I have as my husband's light post, illuminator and influencer, as I carefully walk in my ability to assist in getting my "man" (husband) on the path to his great purpose on the earth.

These are the words I draw strength from during the everyday learning and growing stages of marriage. That doesn't mean we don't have to be careful in our efforts to influence our husbands; rather than the direct approach, we have to draw them out and be strategic! Nagging, being bossy, or being manipulative just won't work. Try to keep in mind the positive reasons you want to persuade your husband and then let that spirit of helpfulness lead to your truth.

Doing or saying nothing just won't work! We have a purpose within our marriages, ladies. As we continue to learn and grow, remember that change is a daily process that will eventually allow us to see our husbands as the men God is calling them to be. So, if we aren't tuned in, plugged in, and dedicated to the things of God, we shall surely fail in this. Our influence will have the opposite effect, causing confusion; and the author of confusion is the devil. "Hey girl!" you might shout. "Are you calling me the devil?" No… but if the red dress fits. Of course, I'm only joking; but in all seriousness, let us begin to look deeper into the inner workings of our men, how they think and how they truly see themselves.

Their self-evaluation is extremely important and it's reflected back in how men show love. Making your husband feel secure, trusted, and appreciated could swing him into a higher level than he ever dreamed; one that could cultivate an environment for success within your marriage. Our intentions should be to influence our men on their path to purpose. If we keep that at the forefront of our minds, it could very well turn our intentions into reality.

Take some time away from focusing on all the things you feel you need from him but aren't getting, and try to imagine what he may be thinking. Some men struggle with feeling inadequate; they'd never say it out loud, but as their wives it's our job to know without being told. That's why it's so important to be consistent in our communication with God, and to allow the Holy Spirit to aid and guide us in dealing with our husbands. I've benefited from that still, small voice inside of me in the midst of a heated debate with my hubby; the voice that advised me to chill before I said something I would regret.

We should begin to focus on how we can use our God-given influence to propel our marriage toward success. Am I advising you to completely forget about what you need and those needs that remain unmet? No. I'm suggesting that you shift focus for now, until later in the chapter 'But you said yes', when I shift back to you and your needs. God won't leave you hanging and neither will I.

Points to Ponder: Go back and review the three major issues described in this chapter. Do you fit in any of these categories? Begin identifying which ones, and then reflect on how it may be currently affecting your marriage

CHAPTER 2

HAPPILY EVER AFTER ONLY EXIST IN FAIRY TALES

It's funny to watch or even read fairytales and how they end with "and they lived happily ever after". Yeah, for three days... and then real life happens! I believe in happily ever after if you're willing to admit that "ever after" stops, and starts again.

Marriage and being happy have to be sought after every day. I knew prior to getting married that one-day I wanted to be in love, married, have beautiful children, and live happily ever after. If you didn't know, I'm telling you now to spare you from feeling furious and bamboozled like I did: "Happily Ever After, only exists in fairytales."

After I married and realized the reality of married life, I felt my parents had left out so much. It seemed everything that I experienced up until then had given me a storybook outlook on what was to really be expected.

I was living in 'La La Land'.

The books, movies, and the lessons that I was taught by the world contributed to my delusion.

It was time that I faced my reality.

Your story will be just that -- your story; it will not mimic anyone else's. There aren't any play books in the world that will give you total insight into your situation and, to be honest, this is a good thing. There is something about good ol' soul searching and the lessons that come out of it that allow us to grow. It teaches endurance and imprints strength within our souls. It's all about being intentional.

Love tends to find us more intentionally than we think. I always tell single ladies that they may not get everything they wanted in a mate, but, if they allow God to direct them completely in this process, they definitely will get what they need. Keyword, "need." Love tends to find us in places that we would have never sought before and with good reason; because what you lack, God created our husbands to be good, or at least better at, and vice versa. The caveat: this only applies if you chose the right partner.

In my marriage, my husband and I were from two different worlds -- one quiet, one loud. One more aggressive, and one more into making decisions with more thought. I was told, "he will never call, he's way too shy." My phone rang one August evening and it sparked something between us. We talked for hours about the things of the world that intrigued us, inspired us, things like music, God, and our future aspirations.

There was no letting go after that moment. Who would want to? He was a breath of fresh air; nothing like any man I had ever encountered, with the exception of my father. He was excited about me, and about what he foresaw God doing with my life. Wow! Thinking back on the beginning of our relationship allows me to relive the excitement and expectation I experienced. He always remained gentle, the calm to my storm; he sent cards, candy, bears, flowers, and letters. These sentiments were so invigorating to my young self. It made me feel sought after wanted and explored -- feelings that should be present in a woman while dating. I was sweet, and dealt with him gently. I inspired, encouraged, and demanded him to chase after every dream that lay dormant. Sounds like some 2000's R&B hit, right?

You see I didn't have the stereotypical presence or theories of subpar marriages lurking around me. Both grandparents had been married 50+ years, and my parents had been married thirty-two years. It wasn't an option to play around with this marriage thing. I remember the day I got engaged; my grandmother saw the excitement and gleam in my eyes as I stared at my diamond engagement ring in awe. She said, "Now Nicee (family nickname) just so you know, we take marriage very serious in this family." My response was, "I mean of course," gazing into the sparkle of my ring. That conversation definitely imprinted the seriousness of marriage in my mind, and in that moment I vowed to take it very seriously. But even being as serious as they come, I was still walking into a marriage with a person who also had his own definition and ideas about marriage from his own personal experiences.

The question of the day is how do you merge the two ideas in order to achieve marital success? My husband's experience had been much different than mine. In our earlier conversations, he shared with me that his parents were never married; and he never had a real relationship with his father. His views of marriage came from what he observed while watching his mother and stepfather, and a very close cousin who was like a mentor to him growing up. These relationships, whether they agree to it or not, helped to shape our perceptions, and influenced decisions within our own marriages. Merging these two perceptions depended on our willingness to cultivate a new, cohesive vision for our own marriage. We built our own vision for our marriage based upon what we experienced from the marriages around us. We decided what things we wanted to take away from those marriages, and what felt didn't belong in our marriage. This is a great tool that really merges two people into one.

I've learned that God enables us to grow even through friction. One day, my husband said to me, "Wow, it's amazing that grass grows even between cracked concrete." I did some research and it turns out that most of these plants that pop up come from a tree source whose roots have branched out and become their own little plant source. It's amazing that although we are a product of our environment, we don't have to stay defined or held hostage by its way of being, thinking, or doing; we can together build our own new positive source and or experience for those that we come in contact with, and have a successfully happy marriage. This is the beauty of growing through friction. It enables us with the opportunity to create a new picture of a successful, happy marriage. We decide what it looks like by two joining together as one to protect the vision. Realistically this breaks that stereotypical belief of happily ever after, and connects the focus to creating a cohesive vision that both of you can create; creating your own picture of what happily every after looks like. This is all about creating a Godly realistic view of meeting one another's needs. It's also about trusting the process of growing together, and abandoning the views of the fairy tale of perfection, and the negative views that we may have been shown in life about marriage. Loving someone is truly about leaving room for growth. It's through the process of friction that we are able to truly withstand the many hard battles that marriages face everyday. It builds an unbreakable bond, and an immense amount of strength within our marriages.

Marriage became real to me on August 9, 2008, when I literally pulled the arm of my father down the aisle to become a wife. You could ask every married woman in the world if they truly knew exactly what they were getting into, and of course we would say "heck no." Marriage is not simplistic at all; it's something that must be fought for every day. Not only do you fight to protect your marriage from failure, but also against the pressures of your own insecurities and fears, that very well shape our personal needs within a marriage. I didn't realize that I was stepping into a boxing match where I would have to fight hard to be the wife that God had called me to be so that I could be put in a position to share with the world.

The first year of marriage whooped my behind, and as I glance back, I see that I made lots of mistakes. I even spoke those words, "I can't do this anymore!" I have a phrase that I say to my girlfriends all the time. "If you haven't said, you can't do this, at least a few times, then I'm not sure you're really in love!"

I'm reminded of our relationship with God, who is in constant pursuit of our affections. He pursues us and loves us, even when we turn our backs on Him. Even when we complain, don't trust, don't honor, and turn our affections away; He still reaches out for us, pulls us in and reminds us: "I love you." Can someone please tell me why we tend to forget to employ these attributes within our own lives when it's our turn? I know. I know, it's hard because... what? You were getting ready to tell me something someone did that would hinder the application of this theory right? Ha!

This is my petition to continue your pursuit. Continue to create moments in love that take your breath away. Laugh, love harder, date, hold hands, and create an environment conducive to love. If there's a spirit of disconnect, or any spirit that speaks against harmony, continue to work on it to create a more loving atmosphere. Find ways to shake things up a bit by introducing new ways to show appreciation to your husband. It starts with the little things. Maybe it's cooking his favorite meal, to something a little more drastic, such as actually having a detailed conversation about his needs, and how you could meet them better. I've had these conversations with my husband ever so often. We humans change over time, and our needs change to. It's important to know your spouse's favorite things. It's important to even know about their sexual desires. We will cover that in the juicy chapter, "The Marriage Sex Talk." Sooner or later, any spirit of strife will have to bow down. Never stop pursuing the affections of the one you love; that is how you win in marriage and create a happily ever after that starts again, and again. .

Points to Ponder: In Colossians 3:2 it states, "Set your minds on things above, not on earthly things. It's important to set our minds on healthy Godly perspective on marital expectations. Start here by writing down a list of some unhealthy expectations that you've noticed that exist in your marriage currently.

CHAPTER 3

BAG LADY

I'm sure most are familiar with the song, "Bag Lady," by singer/songwriter, Erkyah Badu. This song quite eloquently states that, "No man wants a woman showing up to his door with a whole lot of baggage!" Nope, not cute! But, since we live in the real world, it happens. In my case, who I thought I was, and who I really was, ended up being two different people.

I think it's ironic how the very things we don't want people to know about us -- in many instances -- are the very things that are easily detectable. These things may be most detectable to the one you'll call your husband. In past relationships, and even now in my marriage, I began to see broken remnants of myself reflected back to me.

Those broken pieces often guided my decisions, and prompted me to fall into old ways of giving and receiving love. Can we agree that it's hard to keep your eyes on consistently loving the way God loves; especially when we've been beaten down, lied to, cheated on, disrespected, neglected, and -- the list could go on, and on? But there is one thing that was for sure; I wasn't progressing into the woman I knew God was calling me to be. I found myself digressing into this pitiful depiction of a woman who was walking around feeling sorry for herself, disappointed, and ashamed. I thought that every hole in my heart gave me permission to love in any way I felt fit. It made me choose wrong, even where right was the obvious choice.

Here I was, a hater of my very own face. I was painting on makeup, taking a black tar like chemical substance, and applying it to my scalp to attach longer hair to mine, all to cover the ugly I perceived in myself when I looked in the mirror, in the hopes that I'd at least be pleasant in someone else's eyes. Not loving what I saw in the mirror created a wedge between who I currently was, and the woman I needed to be in order to grow efficiently as a wife. These things were my bags, and I carried them right to the door of my marriage.

How many of us do this -- oh so effortlessly -- without thought? It could be past relationships, father/mother issues, abuse, etc., that could cause you to start carrying your own baggage around with you. From relationship to relationship, bag after bag. At some point, we have to find refuge in the truth. What God is cultivating in our hearts is an open opportunity for us to be healed from all past wounds. The truth is that He desires us to be free! So when the one He created you for shows up, you have some room in your heart to accept the challenge to continue to grow and empty out those bags!

So, in walks the one who God created just for me. I wasn't prepared to be stripped down to be rebuilt. I had become pretty self-sufficient. I let go of everything that held me hostage -- self-esteem issues, makeup, weaves, fear -- you name it -- it was like God had decided it was my season of healing and then used my husband-to-be to do it. I removed so many things in my life that had clouded my perspective for years.

The process of rebuilding began to take place. God is constantly reminding us of who He is, and who He created us to be! He reminds us every day that He hasn't forgotten about us, and that His hand is still on our lives. Everything will come to pass; we just need to continue to pursue His purpose and will for our lives.

This is even shown daily through our marriages. God uses relational things that we encounter in our marriages to remind us of His unfailing love for us, and His mission to heal our inner wounds through our spouses. That is exactly what God did for me. He created this man to speak life to those dark places of insecurities just by simply pointing out the beauty in them. I remember worrying so much about how my husband would feel about me going natural with my hair. I was afraid that his reaction would be negative to my already damaged self-esteem. Honestly throughout our entire relationship up until this point I wore weave ninety percent of the time. It was really that bad. So this going natural thing was a really important part of my journey to self- acceptance, and truly loving me without any artificial embellishments. To say the least, the journey was rewarding for our marriage and myself. He loved my natural hair! And actually still doesn't care for weave. Which lead me to the realization that, me wearing the flowing, expensive, weave to impress him from the beginning, never impressed him at all. It just goes to show how God works, and intends to use our marriages to help bring us closer to fulfilling his purpose for our lives.

It's vital that we are open to experiencing these moments with God. It builds our strength up as women, as well as wives and mothers. Only God has completely mapped out the course of our lives, and He knows what's best. He knows where you should be, and when you should be there. If we position ourselves to hear, and communicate effectively with God, we have an opportunity to allow Who He is to show forth in our lives and in our marriages. Our lives should continually show forth the goodness of God, His grace, His mercy, and His love.

How can we protect a man's heart if we continually cause wounds to it? It's so easy to inflict pain on someone else, especially those close to us, when we ourselves are hurting inside. Sometimes we don't even realize that the damaged places inside of us from our past cause us to create strongholds in our mind about our marriage. For me it was that first year of marriage; right when things weren't going my way, I was ready to go. With my mouth I would open up and say it to him, like yeah take that. Knowing that wasn't what I really wanted. In my mind, if you tell him you want to leave, then he will get his act together. This never worked; and instead would always put my husband in a more stubborn mood.

God revealed to me years later something that I would never have known on my own; that because of the loss that my husband had experienced in his life, he had built this hard exterior that caused him to immediately shut down at the mere mention of leaving. God wanted me to see that I needed to be more present in understanding that the unfruitful words I released from my mouth with intentions to get my way, really only reopened wounds from my husbands past. See God created us to be nurturers, and to cultivate an environment within our homes of healing, support, and the space for growth to take form. This once again must begin with a long look in the mirror to find out who you really are after healing takes place, while removing dangerous baggage; and truly own what you said yes to.

The question you may ask is, "Where do I start," or "How do I begin the healing process?" Believe me, I never thought it was possible until I had an encounter with God myself that changed my life forever. God's desire is to remind us that he is the solution. You can heal from past wounds. It starts by accepting the truth that you've been wounded, and owning those feelings. It's ok to acknowledge what was done in the past, and how it has made you feel. What is not ok is allowing those feelings to hold you hostage. You see, it holds you hostage by invading your life. It alters our decision making, the way we relate to our husbands, children, friends, etc. The cycle has to be broken. The bible says in Ephesians 4:22-24 to, "Put off our old self," and then it says, "To be made new in the attitude of your mind." Healing is a decision. Change your mind about how those negative feelings will impact you, and then make the decision to love differently then what you've experienced.

Points to Ponder: Keep in mind that you can't stop there. If necessary, seek out counseling. purchase books, podcasts, and ministerial series that reference healing in bible concordance. Seek out scriptures that line up specifically with the issue (baggage) you're dealing with that will speak specifically to your scenario.

CHAPTER 4

ARE YOU HIS OBSTACLE

Far too often I find myself replaying scenes and conversations in my head. I wonder what would happen if I dealt with my man with gentle hands and encouragement and lifted him up? I wonder what difference it would make if I supported him enough, loved him past my own selfish needs, and if I coaxed him toward HIS own successes? The word "coaxed" means to attempt to influence by gentle persuasion, flattery, etc. Definitely something that women love to be on the receiving end of. But do we give it?

We often think that nagging our husbands will get them to do what we want. But have you ever considered the fact that this notion could actually be pushing them away? If we are not asking ourselves these questions, then who will? If we aren't redesigning our relationships for growth to cultivate a culture of successful marriages for this generation, then I ask you, who will? It's our job -- our mandate -- to enhance our marriages and relationships. It's not about you; it's about "WE." How can we be purposeful as a unit? What is our God-given purpose as a couple? These are the questions that we should continually be asking ourselves on a daily basis. It will aid in allowing the right perspective to take root in our hearts.

In moments when you see your man in pursuit of huge life decisions, you may feel anxiety or frustration concerning change for the next phase in life. This is a teachable moment that means three *things*:

1. *Being supportive with no other intent.*

Yes we know what we need from them, and yes, we like to reiterate it on any given occasion. But God spoke to me and said,

"Have no other intention, other than to hear his heart, and serve him." Trust me, I know what it feels like to wonder why I should give something to someone that I am not receiving from them. It is during these times when you must try to remind yourself of who we are ultimately serving through our marriages -- God. We have an opportunity not only to receive unconditional love from God, but also to give it through our marriages. It says in James 1:21

"21 "So get rid of all uncleanness and the rampant outgrowth of wickedness, and in a humble (gentle, modest) spirit receive and welcome the Word which implanted and rooted [in your hearts] contains the power to save your souls."

This scripture challenges us to start by removing elements that tear down and replace them with words that build up. It says, "Be humble," and urges us to tap into the elements which were instilled in us by God; for God created women to be natural nurturers. The definition of nurturer means to care for, to encourage the growth and the development of. This is serious business, because it's the key to feeling empowered; and that empowerment can elevate you beyond the communication barriers that most couples experience.

As wives, we should start with being gentle with our words, because, once spoken, they cannot be taken back. When we activate those God-given attributes, it cultivates an environment for growth, acceptance, and love.

2. Get motivated to get on your own path. (Is there something in your life that is unfulfilled?)

This is one of my favorites. It gets me excited. I remember the moment I started to embrace my full potential as the woman God was calling me to be. I always believed I was called to do something great, but how on earth would I be able to do all these things that were on my heart? I want you to experience that same feeling, and God wants you to feel that same amazing feeling. If no one has told you, I'm telling you now. You have work to do. God didn't just call you to just be an amazing wife, or to just play the same roles that other women may play. God has a great destiny in mind just for you, if you'll just answer his call. It will be frightening and intimidating, but believe me, you'll regret not at least attempting to open the door to that one idea that nudges at your conscious day after day, month after month, year after year. Don't be idle! Get fulfilled! Put your hands to something that brings you joy, and draws you closer to God's will for your life. Just thinking on the many aspects of a Proverbs 31 woman and all the things she put her hands to, that's our prompting that, as many hats as women wear, God has given us the strength, and the wisdom, (know-how) to get ever more done. Refocus your thoughts, and regain momentum in believing that anything is possible for your life. Sometimes, we lose the passion for our dreams. I believe we become too comfortable in "just being" and not as comfortable in taking risks and trying new things. If you're reading this and have a knot in the pit of your stomach, then I'm talking to you. God wants to use your life to put something on the earth that no one else ever could. Yes, it's that serious. As a wife, we have an added benefit; our lives' mission may correlate or be completely different from our purpose within our marriages. Whichever the case, neither mission should be neglected. Honing in on this area of our lives will give us some free time for ourselves and will also give him time to do what he needs to do.

3. Are you making your relationship an obstacle?

Have you ever heard that you're 'hard to deal with?' Sometimes in marriage we come to a crossroad. It's hard recognizing that our behavioral patterns could be leading us away from acting as one unit. If it were that easy we would all get there fast. But there's something about being in the trenches and digging that would have us acquire such strength that keeps us molded together. This can be even harder when communicating and relating becomes extremely difficult. Being moody, and having a stank -- yes I said, "stank," otherwise known as an attitude -- just communicates a non-verbal cue that further separates us from a solution. Honestly, most men shut down; and if they're smart, they'll ignore and never feed into the toddler like fit. We can sometimes behave this way without even knowing it. I have had the opportunity to sit down with a few older women who had been married for 50+ years and the main trend in their advice was to, "be sweet." It might sound outlandish to pair sweet and attitude together, but it's so much more brave to let love override the feelings which can cloud our view.

Believe me, I have personally struggled in this area. It wasn't until God dealt with my heart and showed me that if I truly desired to be heard, I needed to communicate more effectively. He also reminded me that I wasn't a little girl anymore, and I would need to act like a grown woman in order to yield adult results. Don't make this relationship an obstacle. We in life already have to pilot our way through this cold, cold world; let our marriages be a place of safety and rest. I've looked into the eyes of my own husband in the midst of a disagreement and me in one of my "tudes," and what I realized was that he was not hearing me. What I mean by this is there was definitely a language barrier. Instead of me thinking it would open up his ears, and eyes to hear me, it had the exact opposite effect.

In the midst of these challenges, I've found opportunities to learn, grow, and communicate effectively with this man. I realized that even in those moments that presented a chance to love, nurture, and speak life into my husband's goals, I went on a selfish escapade to get my way.

When this becomes a trend in our marriages, this is when men begin to look at everything dealing with us as an obstacle. And, usually without meaning to, ever so gradually place us right in the slot titled: "my obstacle." No one wants to be looked at as someone's obstacle, especially when they're serving in such a vital role as being a wife. It's easy to forget as we are traveling down this road of life, he too is traveling down the same path. Sometimes the cues they receive from us are totally confusing and misleading. This not only lessens our ability to communicate within our relationship with them, but also in our relationship with God. God is constantly in pursuit of us because He wants to help us in our pursuit to communicate with our husbands. As I said in the opening chapter, God is constantly trying to get His will accomplished on the earth. God wants us as wives to be a consistent reflection of His love, respect, honor, and support; as well as a direct communication channel to and from Him.

Sometimes we miss those moments that were intended to
affirm, grow, and strengthen our relationships. I call them
'teachable moments.' Stop sulking and feeling sorry for yourself
and instead, begin to truly show love and support in
your relationship. Remember, obstacles can be moved over, let go,
and forgotten. IF you want to be a part of his future, do yourself a
favor and stop complaining -- stop hindering, and start supporting.
Dwelling on getting what you want out of the deal can hinder this
perspective, but don't let it because it's key to fully engaging and
devoting ourselves to our husbands. This focus can even allow us
to love from places we never thought we could.

When you don't feel like you have it to give, tap into God's
super-natural power that will carry you through. Jesus tapped into
that strength while he was praying in the Garden of Gethsemane.
Jesus agonized about getting on the cross, but His love for us
superseded His own agony. And Jesus got on that cross and

sacrificed His life for ours. We as wives are not exempt from sacrificing! This is the power of true unconditional love.

Points to Ponder: Review #2 in Teachable Moments. Start by identifying and writing down key things you're doing to stay motivated about your individual purpose. If you don't know God's will or purpose for your life, start by doing an inventory on things you may be passionate about. And begin praying that God reveal His purpose for your life.

CHAPTER 5

KNOW YOUR ROLE

My husband is hilarious sometimes; he uses the popular saying, "know your role" to me as a joke. The very first time he said it, it wasn't such a joke to me. But then God began dealing with me about really "knowing my role!" I love how God will sometimes come in and privately deal with us regarding our personal issues.

Do we really know what it takes to be a good wife? Have you explored the definition, and therefore thought about what the role of a wife looks like? Again, these are questions that we must ask ourselves regularly, revisiting them as the years pass.

Let's take the first wife in the Bible: Eve. This is such a great depiction, which immediately conveys how important our role as a wife truly is. After God created Adam, He then proceeded to create a suitable help-mate (helper). There are two things I want to point out here in this story.

#1 God created us as a "helper, (Genesis 2:18)" We were created to assist the leader, not be the leader. *#2 He created her "suitable,(Genesis 2:18)"* He didn't just create some chick that would do, but someone especially created who would be fitting to the stature of the type of man Adam was. With that said, you were created especially to fit the prestige or value of your husband. This is exactly the picture God desires us to have as our role. We are such an important, vital, intricate piece of our unions. I believe God intended for us to know we were a "helper " and "suitable," to be the wife God created us to be. You have what it takes to get the job done. God created you with everything you need.

God didn't stop there. As He pulled Eve from Adam's side (his rib) isn't it fitting to see how, from a medical perspective, the role of a rib is such an important one? The rib happens to protect the most crucial organ in the body; the heart. Wow! What a necessary role we have as helpers created suitable for our husbands, with a mission to protect his heart; the one thing that keeps blood pumping through the whole body, and keeps us alive!! As we protect our husband's hearts, we are keeping the blood flowing, dreams flowing, ambition flowing, and love flowing. We are needed and have such an important role.

Let's take a look at the Proverbs 31 woman. It describes a woman who was all about service. It starts, before even describing the attributes of this woman, by going straight into her worth and on to where her heart lies, speaking specifically to the role of this woman. It goes on to describe this woman who made purposeful, conscious efforts to rise early every day to serve her family and others. Then, to top it off, because of the type of "suitable" woman she was, her husband even had favor with men.

I really believe that today's society has begun to settle into new ideas and perspective on marriage. In times past, the men were treated as the most important figure in the home. Now things have changed and roles have shifted; some by choice, and others because of circumstances beyond our control. With this new definition of marriage, it may seem as if men are not needed, at least there are some women who are quick to let it be known that they don't need a man. How can a man survive in this culture? How can a man grow up in this? How can he really feel capable of leading a woman who treats him as if she does not need him? It's so important to let our men know we need them! They must be told that their roles in our lives are important, vital to our growth, and to our family success.

It is vitally important to note that we set the atmosphere about how genders interact in our homes, especially because the children in our homes will model what we do more than what we say. This deals with how married women talk to their husbands, but I'm also talking to my single women. If you are single, singlehood is prep time. It's a great time to explore areas in your life that need a Godly adjustment -- one being the role of a wife, what it looks like, and how to do it. This is also a time to pursue a deeper relationship with God that will begin to impart wisdom about becoming and staying a wife. Notice that I said "staying." As wives, if we don't make adjustments as time moves forward, as we go through different stages and developments in our marriages, we can miss the opportunity for growth as a unit and risk having a failed marriage.

Let me tell you, there's nothing like a woman who doesn't know her man's next move, let alone a woman who did not support him through that process. They want to know that we will support them even through their failures. This is a strategic opportunity for a new level of intimacy to transform our marriages. A woman will start looking different to a man when he begins to see her for what she was really created to be -- his help.

So what does it mean to be his, "help?" It means not overpowering, demeaning, or mishandling our husbands, but instead learning to deal with them with gentle and gracious hands; the same treatment we seek from them as refuge from our own issues. Knowing our roles fortifies our marriages, and solidifies us in our role as a wife. Be confident in being a helper. There is nothing demeaning about being the force behind the punch. Knowing our role gives us strength as wives, and empowers our word to assist our husbands on the path toward our purpose as a unit, and a family.

Points to Ponder: Go back and break out the Bible and really dive into Proverbs 31. This would also be a good time to have a conversation with your husband about roles, and who plays what in your household. It's important that everyone is on the same page, and then we can set realistic expectations for our marriages.

CHAPTER 6

TWO IS BETTER THAN ONE

Whenever I have the opportunity to discuss marriage, I always share a very important revelation that God showed me in the early stages of dating my husband. I can recall moments where God lodged in my mind, challenging the way I thought about love. In my dating life before my husband, things never seemed to fit quite right. My dreams, goals, interests and aspirations did not match with any other man. When I met my husband, I realized that he was the man I'd been waiting for; the man God created for me to add to my strength so we could go out and conquer the world together. I found the connection that was strategically designed by God to give purpose to my life.

I remember the first time my husband, then a new

acquaintance, called me on my cell phone. Our very first
conversation went on for hours. We talked about music and our
dreams and we laughed a lot. I remember not wanting the
conversation to ever end. As time progresses I see more and more
of God's strategy and vision for getting me on the course that's
made me the woman I am today.

It never made sense until it was really put into action. A few
years into our marriage my husband lost his job. He had been
working at this company for over ten years. He was devastated;
and as he walked through the door that day and asked me to meet
him in the bedroom, honestly I felt it coming. I had always
encouraged him to finish his degree, and continually mentioned
that he didn't need to settle, that I believed God wanted to do great
things with his life. I saw this from the beginning. As he fell to
his knees grabbing my waist with tears, and fear in his eyes, I felt a
peace. I wasn't afraid at all. I knew we were closer to destiny! I
looked him in the eye and told him to stop crying! I
wholeheartedly believed in the man God gave me, and believed

that God would provide us peace as we encountered this storm. I made my plea that maybe this would be a good time for him to finish that degree. That's exactly what he did! My husband is now a few months from graduating with his Graphic Arts degree. He has also been nominated on a national scale for his graphic work, which has opened the door for our small online t-shirt boutique that has been sold nationwide. He also does the graphic work for my blog, website, and of course this book! See how God works? See how purpose works? The two coming together as one creates destiny!! Our purposes collided, catapulting us into God's purpose for our lives both as a unit, and independently.

It makes perfect sense -- God aligns His will for our lives with that of our intended spouses. They will be there to nurture our gifts, support us as we progress and to reassure us in those moments when we're in doubt. God uses us as a source of wisdom, strength, and inspiration for our spouses. He uses us to get each other to the places that we would be less likely to travel alone because of our fear, doubt and insecurities, those things that plague us as we seek to find our purpose. We should view it as an honor that God would trust us with His most prized possessions. That is why it is so important that we cherish our marriages and view them as gifts from God.

There is great purpose in marriage. As great as it all is, God didn't set us up just to marry the love of our life, have children, work good jobs, and live great lives. There is something more specific He had in mind. God is a master strategist, and He is very intentional. He knew that if He got you with the right person He could use your spouse to get you to your destiny. Let's take the marriage between King Xerxes and Esther, found in the book of Esther in bible. This happens to be one of my favorite love stories in the bible. It speaks to courage, destiny, and influence. Here is Esther, an orphan Jewish girl who found herself in the position to become queen. God in his ever so clever way, set up this young lady's destiny to collide with King Xerxes, who fell in love not only with her beauty, but her willingness to be courageous. Not only did she challenge a woman's role in government, but influenced the likeness of King Xerxes, saving her race of people from annihilation. These two becoming one was vital to a people being eradicated from history. But because of destiny, this marriage put them both on the path towards God's will and purpose for their lives.

This is why it is key that we follow His prompting when it comes to choosing a mate. In order for certain things to grow, they must take place in the proper environment. It's scientifically proven that certain plants cannot produce fruit in certain climates; you can wait weeks, even months, but the plant will not bear any fruit. However, when you put something in the proper environment, watch it grow and mature. It progresses God's plan, and that is why it's so important that we women are confident in our ability to blend our lives with our husbands. We have an opportunity to support our husband's growth; we play a vital role in their successes and failures. We support, encourage and motivate them to get on the path toward their purpose. It's important to be keyed into the specific needs of YOUR man.

NOBODY should know your man better than you.

As two become one with marriage, we begin the journey of creating an atmosphere in our households that cultivates growth. Our purposes begin to merge. When I say merge, I don't mean they begin to look the same, but that they become a cohesive unified force. Our marriages should be unstoppable forces put together to change the world in whatever way that may be. If God can bring together two, He can create a movement. Whatever one lacks, it may be a source of strength for the other, enabling support and growth. In Mark 10:8 it reads, " And the two shall become one flesh, so they are two and no longer one (New International Version)." God's intention for marriage was to bring us together to become one.

It's in the *becoming* that we build and surround ourselves with a vision for love and empowerment to have one sound, one voice. The becoming is a pursuit; a pursuit of one that will take you around many mountains until you get the point. Come together, become one, because two is better than one.

Points to Ponder: Write down and reflect on the moment you experienced you and your husband coming together as one. Reminiscing on those moments allow space for new ones to be created. Use that memory as fuel to then recreate another opportunity for you and your husband to directly sync.

CHAPTER 7

PROTECT YOUR THOUGHT LIFE

The mind, from the very beginning, is where we build our

preconceptions about marriage. Our thoughts need to be protected

from negative influences that could oppose God's intent for our

marriages. Further, our thoughts are also where God subtly rests

his expectations for what type of wives he is calling us to be. If we

aren't careful, we can allow our minds to create and house

thoughts that contradict God's plans for us. It is up to us to tack

down within our own thought lives the positive God-driven

attributes of marriage that we desire to have. In my premarital

years, I always found myself studying and reading the bible to get

a solid picture of what a wife was to be, and now, even after being

married for eight years, I still go back to the word to continue my

plight to grow as a Christian married woman. I've also attributed

writing down my thoughts in a hand written journal, and a journal app that I have downloaded on my phone. It's a consistent pursuit to grow as a wife, ones knowledge will continue to grow, and grow. That's why it's important that we continue to create avenues of which we are getting consistent substance in, and getting wounds out (Quick Tip: Reading the Bible, Marriage self help literature, and journaling).

If our desire as wives is for faithfulness, patience, love and forgiveness to be alive in our marriages, then these should be the concepts we focus our thoughts and actions on daily. Philippians 4:8 says, "Finally, brothers and sisters, whatever is true, whatever is noble, whatever is right, whatever is pure, whatever is lovely, whatever is admirable--if anything is excellent or praiseworthy-- think about such things." If you believe that being faithful, patient, loving, and forgiving are actions that you want to be alive in your marriage, create a space in your mind that caters to activating such thoughts. Think and do, think and do. In order for an action to be activated, it must be a thought first; thoughts are then put into action. It's simple; give what you want to receive. Give it with no other intent. The intent should be emerged in serving this man with everything God put in you. Don't worry about what he is doing. Let God handle that! I know it may sound cliché, but God truly is the only advocate that will work on our behalf in really breaking down the psyche of a man. Let God do the work, and you follow His prompting.

If we can get our thoughts together about our marriages, and ourselves, then things will begin to come together. In my case, when I changed my thoughts about my marriage it enabled another level of trust to develop between God and me. That trust enabled me to allow God to fight my battles. I went to God first about certain issues between my husband and I that I knew only God could remedy, because one human being doesn't have the power to change another person. I'm not saying your emotional pleas to him won't have an effect, but, believe me, it was God, not you, that was the driving force.

All of this will take some work and it will not be easy. There are elements surrounding us which contribute to the demise of positive thoughts concerning our marriages; whether from social media, popular television shows, or those "girlfriends" close to you. It's important that we not just ignore these negative influences to retain a Godly perspective on marriage, but speaking up, and out about God's word about them. How dare we stand by and let these worldly views destroy the platform God has built for us to stand on. It saddens me to see wives live out these new relationship views that leave them empty, emotionally wrecked, and still searching for the purpose in love. It leaves a stigma around marriage that makes it completely unappetizing; but if we keep our thoughts and hearts convinced of God's purpose, we can refute this negative picture of marriage. In viewing illustrations of these theories on television shows and social media, I have found that there are some trends about marriage typically portrayed in the media.

The first social media theory up is the idea of the hall pass, which is a concept promoted on television shows, social media, and also the name of a widely released movie. A hall pass is when one partner gives the other permission to temporarily step outside of their marriages. The Bible, in 2 Corinthians 10:5 (NIV) says, "We demolish arguments and every pretension (or thoughts) that sets itself up against the knowledge of God, and we take captive every thought to make it obedient to Christ." This means any pretension or thought that comes to negate what God spoke into existence for marriage must be taken captive, and then put into the category of, "not OK." Marriage was designed to be between one woman, and one man. I don't know about you, but I am not hip to sharing my husband, nor do I think this lifestyle should be glorified. The Bible is clear about adultery, which is defined as sexual intercourse between a married person and person who is not their spouse. In Proverbs 6:32, it reads, "But a man who commits adultery lacks judgment; whoever does so destroys himself (NIV). That same standard stands for us women, too. Does God cheat on us? Is God fully committed to loving, pursuing, protecting, and providing his love to us? If the marriage covenant mirrors God's relationship with his people, then our commitments within our marriage should be as such.

As a married woman, these are notions that we battle on the front lines everyday. In order for us to win the battle in our minds, we have to eliminate these theories. It's enough to battle with our own self esteem, trying to convince ourselves that we are good enough, pleasurable to our husband's eyes; but to then have to put all of that at risk by feeling pressured to share the one man promised to us by God, will inevitably cause us to forfeit the promise and purpose of the marriage God is calling us to experience. You can read the word, and quote the scripture, but it will stop you dead in your tracks if you continue to view and take in that junk. I understand for some it just may not affect them, but for others, you're literally tortured by these foolish ideas. If you find yourself struggling in this area, detach yourself from certain television shows, social media sites, and post that put you at risk. I learned that when battling issues in the mind, it's important to be dogmatic about filtering your ear and your eye gate. Stop watching, listening, and hanging out with any source that teaches these ideas.

The next theory is the Social Media Stalker. Have you ever glanced at your husband's Facebook, Twitter, or Instagram news feeds? Do you have all the passwords, and check them daily? Have you ever become paranoid at the mere thought of your husband even being fond of another woman's beauty? Social media is ridden with so many opportunities for our husbands, but marital happiness begins and ends with trust. Point, blank, and the period. If you don't trust him then why did you marry him? This was the most important thing to remind myself to keep me rooted in the reasons I married my husband in the first place -- to reassure me of the strong character he had displayed from the very beginning. What I do is focus on positive thinking and thoughts by taking any worry or anxiety to God, and checking my motives. I know you may be wondering what I mean by that. I check my motives to make sure that these thoughts aren't being driven by some foolish, unproductive quandary to soothe my self-esteem.

Please check yourself at the door, and make sure that this isn't you. If anything questionable ever comes up, I then take it to my husband respectfully. The rest is up to my husband and whether he'll make the decision to follow the guidance from the Holy Spirit and God in situations that may be questionable. Remember that the marriage covenant is a mirrored image of God's covenant to his people; it speaks to God's commitment and promises to us, one of which is to be faithful and trustworthy. What better way to show forth God's love than by trusting our husbands. There should be no reason to snoop without our husbands permission.

I remember one Sunday afternoon sitting on the couch with my husband, watching an episode of a very popular television show. My husband, who was working on his computer and glancing up in intervals, finally stopped what he was doing and fixated on the screen. He said, "Wow, she is very pretty." I don't know if it was the "very" that threw me off or just hearing my man speak of the beauty of another woman; a woman beautiful enough to completely take his focus from what he was immersed in. This situation brought me to a place of reflection. Who was I really? Did I like who I was when I looked at myself in the mirror? Honestly, did I really believe I was beautiful, flaws and all? It's funny, realistically a man will never understand the psyche of woman or the dangerous roads we travel down to even begin to bring ourselves full circle. It's a journey and a process for a woman to even begin to challenge the way she thinks of herself, let alone deal with the thoughts and opinions of others. Social media can be a danger zone for a woman who does not know who she is or who needs to be affirmed. If we only knew that what we think of ourselves is broadcasted through our actions. We choose the behavior that will follow, for ourselves and how others will behave towards us.

Now let's be clear, I generally don't have jealous tendencies, but this was a learning moment for me. My reaction was similar to how I think many women would behave -- a sharp glance in his direction. Even the most confident, well put-together women mentally and physically battle with their own self-perceptions. It's so important that we are truly honest with ourselves. If you feel jealous, it's OK to address how you feel about the situation, but make sure that you don't allow your insecurities to guide your expectations for his behavior.

You have to take the lead on your thoughts by actively putting things in place to combat behaviors as well. They can be positive or negative, but the more we surround ourselves with God's positive influences we can continually beat these thoughts, and ideas. Join positive wives blogs, pick up a good book, get involved in your local church wives ministry, and surround yourself with great-married women who are passionate about their marriage, too. This is how we continually fight the battle in our minds.

Points to Ponder: Protecting your thought life is going to take extreme measures. Use this time to put in place an,

"Accountability Partner." Other than your husband, find a close

friend, or family member that you trust that you can link up with in

moments where you may be struggling with a thought.

Accountability partners assist in holding you responsible to

operating in your new way of thinking. Make sure that this doesn't

turn into a gossip session.

CHAPTER 8

THE MARRIED SEX TALK

Ok, come on in, have a seat. Can someone please tell me why Christians are so afraid to talk about sex? Married or not, it should be a topic that one is well-versed in, within Godly parameters of course. We as Christians should know the true essence for which "sex" was created. I understand it can be a very private matter, but when we are talking about marital issues, all cards must be on the table.

I have a question for you married folk, "Are you having sex?" I hope you said yes! I can recall a recent visit to my doctor for an annual visit. As she ran down her list of questions, one happened to be, "Are you sexually active?" In my head I was wondering why on earth would she even ask me that. I mean, a glance at my chart made it obvious I was married and had two young children. I thought that made the answer to her question pretty obvious. So, my answer was, "Well I am married." She replied, "What does that mean? Everyone who is married is not having sex." I couldn't fathom being married and not being sexually active with my husband. I mean, we had waited our whole lives to be intimate, why would we not take advantage of the opportunity?

As much as one would like to think it's unimportant, I'm here to share that's just not the case. In my early years of marriage, my eyes became open about sex and its vital importance within a marriage; it's about so much more than just being fruitful and multiplying. I really believe that the enemy detests married people coming together to *know* one another sexually. It's a level of intimacy that can expose Satan's lies. It can even expose his plans to divide the two of you. Sex was created by God, exclusively reserved for a husband, and a wife. This act of sacrificial giving of one's body for the good and pleasure of another, is a shadow of Jesus' giving of his own body for the love and sake of his Bride, the church.

Have you ever had a moment where you were upset with your spouse, but then the strong desire to reconcile turns into a passionate intimate session of sex? Are you uncomfortable yet? If so, I don't apologize it's time to get real about your married sex life! I've been there; extremely upset with my husband, and emerged in the, "I'm not talking to you," game. Don't leave me out there; I know I'm not alone. You see in most instances some men completely forget what happened by the end of the day anyway. I know my husband does. I'm still mad, and come bedtime, I snuggle up to my side of the bed (with the don't you dare touch me, and this will go on until you make it right face.) He leans over to pull me close, but I turn him away. You see, the plan in our heads is to hold out (not having sex with our husbands) until we feel they've served their time in the, "Dog house." Withholding sex from our husbands isn't doing you or him any favors and it sure isn't pleasing to God. I'll admit, I've tried it, and honestly, it only truly exposed my desire to really want to have sex. Sex should never be put in the category of a chore. Just as women desire to be wanted sexually within a marriage, so do men. I encourage you to spice up the romance within your marriage and to pursue one another as you did in the very beginning stages.

It's important that we have conversations with our spouses about what their sexual needs are. I have these conversations with my husband often. It boils down to committing to exploring his sexual needs, and vice versa, or accepting that you may be leaving the door open for him to seek sexual fulfillment elsewhere. If you are uncomfortable with some of his sexual needs, find a compromise or a happy medium.

Ladies, we need to stop thinking we are doing our husbands a favor by having sex with them. Let's be honest, we enjoy it too. And if you're reading this and cringing at the idea of exploring your sexual relationship with your husband because you're not interested in sex, you should definitely see which bag you're holding on to from the earlier chapter called Bag Lady, which could help you figure out where these feelings could be coming from. If you desire to be with this man and be free in your sexual relationship with him, do yourself a favor and seek out counsel to explore what might be causing you to be uninterested in sex.

The beginning years of marriage are usually filled with sex, and lots of it. But as the years fly by, and children, along with other responsibilities, come into the picture, our lives get hectic. Sex slowly becomes that last thing on our list. It has to be a priority; it has to be! I decided to take my sex life with my husband into my own hands; I wanted him to feel like I desired and wanted him. Remember, men want to feel desired too. As I began to pursue him, he pursued me. It became a fun, a flirting game that had us awaiting each other's advances. It allows another level of intimacy to develop. I found myself letting go of small disputes and disagreements that didn't even matter to me anymore. Upgrading our sex life put me in a whole new mind space. If enjoyed, sex can be used as a weapon against the enemy's plots and schemes against our marriages. Sex becomes a powerful tool when used from a defensive perspective. Being on the defense means aggressively seeking to upgrade your sex life with your husband. To continue efforts to keep a deep intimate connection. The enemy hates this! The moment a husband and wife connect on another level, it opens the gate for purpose to erupt. That purpose changes the world in whatever capacity that may be, considering why God brought the two of you together. This also means having those difficult conversations that intimately connect us to our spouses. We should be having these conversations. We should be seeking in prayer ,along with our spouse, how we can be connected deeper through sexual intimacy (in-to-me-see).

This isn't time to start acting all shy, and timid. If you want to keep this man's mind tuned into you sexually, it's time to start actively seeking tools to upgrade your married sex life. Start with the checklist:

✓ *Have a Face –to- Face conversation about each others sexual desires. Be*

specific about what you need and how it
makes you feel. If necessary take notes
to refer back to.

✓ Don't be afraid to try new things that
may bring pleasure to your spouse. If
it's something that makes you
uncomfortable, try a happy medium.

✓ Make sex a priority. Yes things will
come up that may put sex with your
spouse last on the list, but it's up to us to
make a conscious effort to get back to it.

✓ Clear out your mind space that may be
blocking you from connecting with your
spouse during sex. It's easy for our
minds to go different places with our
hectic lifestyles, stay focused during sex.
Focus on tapping into your passion and
desire to be please, and be pleased.

✓ HAVE SEX, lots of it!

This checklist gives a few points on where you can begin to explore your married sex life. No more stigmas around it, just two people under covenant with God, seeking to enjoy one another sexually; this pleases God.

There also is another part to this whole married sex talk that many don't even dive into. I would have to ask this question: "Are you bringing other people to bed with you?" This topic carries over into our sex life from our baggage dealt with in, "Bag Lady," once again. Some may think I'm making sexual innuendos, but this is predicated on past sexual relationships that affect the way we sexually connect with our spouse. This connection can be severely damaged every time we willingly gave our self sexually to someone other than our husbands. In many cases this is something that occurred prior to getting married. I know sexual purity is off the map these days, and just viewed as a religious concept that many don't ,and won't, live by. You see, God is always trying to protect us; this is one of the very instances. It says in 1 Corinthians 6:18, to flee from sexual immorality, it goes on to say that it leads you to sin against your own body. What does this mean? Sinning against your own body connects us to our sexuality, and the places that it connects us to that affect us mentally, physically, emotionally, and spiritually. These are direct connections God intended to sync us with our husbands. God intended for it to be an uninterrupted connection. But when we choose to forgo his plan, it builds a communication barrier that can rear its ugly head in our marriage bed. It can cause confusion. You'll find yourself comparing your ex lover with your husband, mixed up about your needs, untrusting of going deeper sexually because you feel the need to still protect yourself. Just wounded. But God offers his healing through his blood, ALREADY shed for your mind to break free.

Not only do past sexual relationships hinder our marital sex life, but so may sexual abuse and molestation. These images from the past are replayed in the mind of a woman, building up a stronghold overtime. A stronghold is a thought, or belief, that comes in the form of an argument and or reasoning about what you believe. In this instance it wants to effect you negatively by arguing or reasoning in your mind, causing you to live in guilt and shame about your past abuse.

It leaves you ashamed of your own body, ashamed of sexual desires, and confused about God's original intent for sex (God commands that sexual relations between a man and woman are to be only within the institution of marriage). These thoughts then leak over into your married sex life. It's important to know that your experience was perverted, causing you to view sex, or the usage of sex incorrectly, and that's not what God ever intended. This can make it extremely hard to be intimate with your husband. These strongholds try and stop the healing process, building up a wall in your mind that distorts God's biblical views about sex. It's important to view these occurrences as a hindrance to your sexual freedom, personal healing, and growth. It's important to be free with our husbands. You can't fully give yourself to your husband sexually with these weights holding unto you. In order for healing to begin to take place, start with these tools:

1. Open the bible and revisit Gods original intent for sex (Genesis 1:27-, and how circumstances that occur in our life may cause confusion, but doesn't take away from God's original intent.

2. Forgive the abuser; unforgiveness further more digs our hearts into a deeper hole. You can't fully love from a broken heart. Forgiveness frees you. In most instances, abusers go on with their lives carefree, happy; and you're left stuck! Take this baggage, unpack it, and let God be your avenger.

3. Open your heart for extensive healing. Don't hide, but unleash it all. Start by diving into God's word and read scriptures that talk about healing (Isaiah 41:10, Matthew 11:28, Psalms 30:2, Psalms 41:2-3, and many more). Mediate on these day and night.

If you remember from, "Bag Lady," I stated the process of breaking free starts with recognizing that there is even an issue existing, and working against the well being of your marriage. The steps to true healing begin with prayer, and connecting yourself to God. Literally, not just the act of laying those wounds down is enough, but actually doing it.

Let's remember with our fight to freedom and healing we have to know who, and what we are wrestling with. In Ephesians 6:12 it says, "For we are not fighting against flesh-and-blood enemies, but against evil rulers and authorities of the unseen world, against mighty powers in this dark world, and against evil spirits in the heavenly places (NLT)." This scripture lets us know that what we aren't fighting the physical people or situations that hurt us, but against the powers that intend to contradict who God is calling us to be. He created us whole, complete, and lack nothing. It's the enemies plan to use the issues we face as a way to distract our thoughts and leave us hurt, depressed, unfocused, and miserable about our past. The enemy wants you to stay bound to your pain.

But I'm hear to inform you that, NO MA'AM you are FREE, whole, and complete. And God has given you the right to move forward, and create sexual intimacy with your husband that is so amazing!

If you haven't already, write out those feelings from those past wounds, and with your word in hand literally lay those things out in front of the word as an act of actually laying those burdens before God, casting your cares upon him. It says in 1 Peter 5:7, "Cast all your anxiety on him because he cares for you." God doesn't want to see you bound, or see your marriage held up because you can't get over a wound from a relationship that is long over. This is the opportunity for growth, and the opportunity to magnify the greater picture of your true undoubted connection with the man you love. Do whatever you need to do to break the cycle. If it's counseling, reading, and studying the word this is the fast track to breaking free sexually with your husband.

Points to Ponder: Sit down with your husband and ask him specifically about his sexual needs. Make sure that you ask him to be very specific so that you can explore some things that you may want to try in order to upgrade your married sex life. Be sure to give yours, too.

CHAPTER 9

BUT YOU SAID YES

Can we be completely honest? Would you agree that some of us, in saying "yes," might have eagerly agreed to something that we weren't completely ready for? Our minds and hearts couldn't even fathom the immense amount of pressure and pruning that would take place before we would become the wife that God has called us to be. It's a never-ending process, and a never-ending opportunity to evaluate where you are and make the necessary adjustments.

You said yes; so with that, you agreed to doing the work it takes to continue on this journey toward growth, because that is exactly what marriage is. It's always changing, shifting and rearranging, all about learning someone once, and then again, and then again. But it really boils down to this, "You said yes!" I

know that you may grow weary in the process, because I know I

have. Your marriage can start out with such passion and pursuit

and then it seems you lose the urge to continue to pursue one

another's affections. Who you are at year one is so different than

who you are at year five. What is required in terms of how to

interact relationally, emotionally, sexually, etc. will change during

the course of those years, and years to come.   We must continue to

make the shift, and all the changes required to get our marriages on

board with God's purpose for them.

It's just like a plant in a garden that needs consistent care.

God is available 24 hours a day, 7 days a week, and 365 days a

year to feed you the proper nourishment. We have been created

with the tools to keep nourishing our marriages to health whenever

needed. God is always right there for you, providing the necessary

strength, support and wisdom whenever you're willing to take

ahold of it. It's up to us as married individuals to do the work on

ourselves and to work as a unit with our spouses in order to enable consistent growth. It's all for the glory of God; an opportunity to be pursued by God to actively engage your life. God's plan through our marriages is to put us on a path to our destiny.

Marriage is a continuous journey, always growing and evolving. It's important to stay consistent with identifying the reasoning behind what we do, because out of that arises a lesson, one that generally gives us insight on what God is doing and what's to come. I find myself coming to this crossroads often; one where God is constantly reminding me of who I am and who I could be if I surrendered every area of my life to Him. Not just for peace in my marriage, but for peace within myself. It's like you're one shot away from hitting the winning shot in the game, one step closer to God's purpose for your life. God is willing to use whatever He has, to get us to see that, the women we are, are enough. We are enough to identify the issues and struggles and adjustments that shift our focus away from walking freely in love.

When you said "yes," you may not have known all that you said yes to at the moment. But, hopefully, you intended to learn to offer, and learn unconditional love at it's best. Ask yourself if you'll love past your current circumstance and stand up and fight for love. I had the pleasure of watching and taking in a heap of knowledge about marriage by watching my grandmother for the last 10+ years care for my grandfather, a victim of a stroke that left him unable to fully care for him self. Day after day, week after week I watched this tiny woman administer care to this man; feeding, clothing, bathing, even trying to physically lift him, until the day he died. We say the vows, in sickness and in health, for better or for worst, till death do us part. But do we really mean it? How far are you willing to sacrifice? It may not be an illness; it could just be an unmet need for unconditional love. Love is a sacrifice! At some point we have to realize that it is not about us! But more about how we can show the love of God to the one God created to be loved by us.

We said yes to giving parts of ourselves that we didn't even know existed. We said yes to loving someone through his issues, and supporting him through becoming the man God called him to be. It's important to know that we are never given an exact date when our husband will arrive at his final calling and transformed into the man he was meant to be. One reason the Bible gives us for this is that it helps to test and strengthen our faith in God's promise. In Philippians 2:12 (American Standard Version) it says, "So then, my beloved, even as ye have always obeyed, not as in my presence only, but now much more in my absence, work out your own salvation with fear and trembling," The question that remains is, do you trust God? Do you trust God's plan for your life? I found myself asking this question and allowing it to motivate me to do the work. God granted me the opportunity to live out my destiny, and, make mistakes along the way that would cause pain, but also lead to growth. Now that's grace! What if our husbands will never be able to love us the way we WANT them to? Maybe that's because what God has planned to do *through* our husbands is much greater than we could even fathom. God always has a plan, and can use the unassuming for his glory to be revealed in our lives.

It took me sitting down and reflecting on God's goodness and mercy, to bring me to the realization that I hadn't been exhibiting the qualities of a wife that God had called me to. Here God offered me a young man full of hopes and dreams, one who didn't have the benefit of seeing examples of successful marriages throughout his life like I did. There I was, just expecting this man to know what to do; it's truly a blessing that God was working on the inside of my husband, manifesting his abilities even without the benefit of an upbringing full of positive marital role models. God makes up the difference. All God was asking me to do was support my husband and love him toward his purpose. That is why this marriage thing is not for everyone. Of course, the situations and circumstances of each marriage will vary, but it's compassion and purpose that will prevail if enacted. When that yes was given, most women thought of what and who this man would become. That's what the excitement is all about -- unwrapping this mysterious box to unveil what beautiful surprise that awaits inside.

When you fight for it, love is such a beautiful surprise; but whatever you're seeking for your marriage should start with you. Remember that what you said yes to will challenge you and push you into becoming a pretty powerful woman who will be used by God to help affirm and speak life into God's gift; your husband. Now that's what you said yes to.

Let's end this with a prayer:

Heavenly Father, together with women all over the world, we stand together to acknowledge that we are loved, chosen, called, equipped, powerful, women with a purpose built by you. You've built us with the knowledge, the strength, and the possibilities to stretch beyond our norms, to extend our hearts and minds far beyond our limits. We pray that you continue to challenge our hearts, and heal EVERY broken place that may try to distract our confidence in you. Continue to enable us to understand that our pain and our disappointments, feed our drive, and motivation to pursue Your purpose for our lives. Lord even in the darkest places in our lives, we are asking for light. We come

against any forms of depression, anxiety, worry, shame, defeat,

fear, hurt, unforgiveness, lack, theories, and division that may try

and take residence in our hearts, and minds. For we know that NO

weapon formed against SHALL be able to prosper. We trust you,

and believe that we WILL rise to be women of great destiny. We

pray that you will continue to guide, keep, and protect us from any

hurt, harm, danger, sickness, and disease. We speak an

abundance of love, joy, peace, and passion to erupt in our lives

this very moment.

And God we lift our marriages up to you. We are thankful

for the love you have created for us. We pray that you will

continue to allow our marriages to flourish. Bless them; protect

them against any threats of dissention that does not bring about

healing, and growth. Lord we ask that a NEW level of intimacy

explode within our marriages. We pray for the courage to love

unconditionally. We pray to KNOW our husbands intimately to

fulfill their desires. We pray that as we follow You, you will guide us as we encourage our husbands pursuit towards purpose. Let Your will be done in our lives, and through our marriages. In Jesus mighty name we pray, AMEN.

The fight is on! Love you!! Shanise L. Ollie

Shanise L. Ollie

But You said, "Yes"